Making Your Money Grow

Time-saving books that teach specific skills to busy people, focusing on what really matters; the things that make a difference – the *essentials*. Other books in the series include:

Making Great Presentations

Speaking in Public

Responding to Stress

Succeeding at Interviews

Solving Problems

Hiring People

Getting Started on the Internet

Writing Great Copy

Making the Best Man's Speech

Writing Good Reports

Feeling Good for No Good Reason

Making the Most of Your Time

For full details please send for a free copy of the latest catalogue.
See back cover for address.

The things that really matter about

Making Your Money Grow

John Whiteley

ESSENTIALS

Published in 2000 by
How To Books Ltd, 3 Newtec Place,
Magdalen Road, Oxford OX4 1RE, United Kingdom
Tel: (01865) 793806   Fax: (01865) 248780
email: info@howtobooks.co.uk
www.howtobooks.co.uk

British Library Cataloguing in Publication Data.
A catalogue record for this book is available from
the British Library.

Edited by Barbara Massam
Cover design by Shireen Nathoo Design
Cover copy by Sallyann Sheridan
Produced for How To Books by Deer Park Productions
Typeset by PDQ Typesetting, Newcastle-under-Lyme, Staffordshire
Printed and bound in Great Britain

NOTE: The material contained in this book is set out in good faith for general guidance and no liability can be accepted for loss or expense incurred
as a result of relying in particular circumstances on
statements made in the book. Laws and regulations are complex
and liable to change, and readers should check the current position
with the relevant authorities before making personal arrangements.

ESSENTIALS *is an imprint of*
How To Books

Contents

Preface   **7**

1 Defining your objectives   **8**
Thinking about your needs   9
Defining your objectives   9
Reviewing your objectives   10
Deciding on income, capital, or both   10
Keeping your plans flexible   11
Keeping your wits about you   11

2 Evaluating the risk/reward relationship   **13**
Understanding the risks   14
Judging the risk profile   15
Spreading the risk   17
Balancing the risk/reward equation   17

3 Tackling the stock market   **19**
Dealing in stocks and shares   20
Choosing a stockbroker   21
Getting your portfolio managed   21
Understanding the index and reading the prices   22
Spotting a good thing   23

4 Choosing a collective investment   **25**
Understanding the format   26
Joining an investment club   28
Choosing a fund   28

5 Investing in your country   **32**
Knowing why to invest in government stocks   33
Knowing how to invest in government stocks   34
Understanding National Savings   36

6 Planning for your retirement   **39**
Joining a superannuation scheme   40
Taking out a personal pension plan   40

Choosing a policy   41
Taking the benefits   42

7   Benefiting from incentives   44
Benefiting from tax breaks   45
Getting shareholder concessions   47

8   Investing in property   48
Investing in commercial and industrial property   49
Investing in residential property   49
Investing in holiday lettings   50
Realising the value in your home   50

9   Playing on the edge   53
Investing ethically   54
Collecting for pleasure and profit   56
Dealing in commodities   58
Trading in derivatives   58

10 Taking advice   61
Knowing when to use an adviser   62
Knowing what to ask   62
Knowing who to choose   63

Preface

Do you feel that the world of savings and investments is too full of jargon, and you cannot break through the mystique? This is the book for you.

This book is for ordinary people who want to be in control of their own financial destiny. It was born out of a conviction that ordinary people can successfully implement their own saving and investment strategy. All that is needed is a grasp of the basic principles.

This book does not promise to make you rich overnight. However, it seeks to guide you through what might seem like a jungle by keeping in mind your objectives – and prompting you to keep those objectives under constant review.

John Whiteley

1 Defining Your Objectives

Without an aim you will not achieve anything worthwhile – this applies as much to savings as anything else.

6 things that really matter

1 **THINKING ABOUT YOUR NEEDS**

2 **DEFINING YOUR OBJECTIVES**

3 **REVIEWING YOUR OBJECTIVES**

4 **DECIDING ON INCOME, CAPITAL, OR BOTH**

5 **KEEPING YOUR PLANS FLEXIBLE**

6 **KEEPING YOUR WITS ABOUT YOU**

If you were to shoot an arrow at a blank wall, you could then paint a target round the spot it hit, and claim to have hit the target dead centre. Many people try to run their lives – and their savings – this way. If you do not plan well in advance, you may succeed in putting aside some money in a savings account, but it goes no further.

Take time to think about your needs, and your life plans. Only then can you define your objectives. Don't stop there! Keep your plans under constant review so that they meet your changing needs.

If you have no purpose for your savings, they can too easily get used up on the first emergency, or even the first whim, that comes along.

IS THIS YOU?

 • *I would like to save enough to put a deposit on a house.* • *My retirement is fast approaching, and I don't know how I am going to make ends meet.* • *I would really like to buy a car. Should I get it on HP, or save up for it?* • *I have tried saving, but I don't have enough discipline to keep it up regularly.* • *I want my children to inherit my wealth, and not have it swallowed up by death duties. Do I give it all away now? If so, what am I going to live on?*

 THINKING ABOUT YOUR NEEDS

Your first task is to sit down and think about your **needs**. This will help you to structure your savings and investments. Imagine you have a certain sum in your bank account – say, £20,000.

- What would you do with it?
- What are your needs and desires?
- What would have to be paid immediately?
- What is less urgent?
- When will your needs materialise?

For example, if you want to save for your retirement, put your savings where you cannot touch them until you retire. Otherwise, you might use the money for something else, and find yourself short when you come to retire.

Before you do anything sit down and think about your needs.

 DEFINING YOUR OBJECTIVES

Once you have decided what you needs are, define your **objectives**. Do it in writing, and be as specific as you can, in terms of time span, and amounts involved. For example:

- In five years' time I want to have saved £10,000 to put down as a deposit on a house.

You may find you have several objectives. If so, rank them in order of **priority**. Don't shirk this one.

Always formalise and prioritise you objectives. The most urgent things are not necessarily the most important.

 REVIEWING YOUR OBJECTIVES

As a young person, you may want to save up for a sports car, or the latest in windsurfing gear. Then you marry and you want to buy a house. Children come along, and you think about their education. In middle life, you are increasingly concerned about providing for retirement. At last you retire, and now you want to supplement your income from your savings. Some years into retirement, you may think about passing on your wealth.

At all times, be aware of your **changing circumstances**, and plan your savings with them in mind. Changes usually happen slowly, and we do not always recognise them. Therefore, take time regularly – say every five years – to review where your life is going. Then make any changes necessary.

Don't let things drift. Make a definite date in your diary to review your circumstances and your objectives.

 DECIDING ON INCOME, CAPITAL, OR BOTH

Many people use their accumulated savings to generate an income, to supplement the basic state pension. If this is your aim, invest your savings in a form which will generate this income for you. Bear in mind the effect of inflation, and try to obtain from your savings an income that has at least the possibility of escalating year by year.

Inflation can have a devastating effect on your capital. This is particularly relevant in planning for retirement. Start saving for retirement as early as possible.

Your retirement may be 30 or 40 years away, but your savings would be seriously eroded over that period. Therefore your **main objective must be to save in a form that protects you against inflation.**

You may want an income from your savings and to protect the capital. Certain investments purport to do that, but they inevitably represent a compromise of some kind.

Make sure you know the difference between income and capital – and never use capital to top up your income.

 KEEPING YOUR PLANS FLEXIBLE

Unless you are endowed with second sight, you do not know what the future holds. One in three marriages ends in divorce, and a divorce upsets the best planned savings and investment strategy. There are many things which can cause your plans to go awry, such as redundancy or ill health.

Always try to make your savings as **flexible** as possible. Ask questions about any investment you undertake:

- Can I unscramble it or encash it if necessary?
- Is the value liable to fall as well as rise?
- Can I pass it on easily to my descendants?

Nothing is certain in this life except change. Be ready for it.

 KEEPING YOUR WITS ABOUT YOU

There are hundreds, even thousands of investment opportunities, and choosing the one to suit you could be difficult. There are sharks out there – and even the ones which are not dodgy may not be the right ones for you.

Bear in mind some simple guidelines.

- If you do not understand something, keep away from it. **Don't go for anything that is more complicated than you like**. The simpler it is, the more flexible you can be.

- Ask yourself common-sense questions – Does it add up? Can I see what my money is being used for? Is the return offered out of line with the going rate?

- Find out as much as you can about the investment. Get as much as you can from the investment provider. Then get independent information.

Remember: Keep it simple. If a proposal seems too good to be true, it probably is. You cannot have too much information.

MAKING WHAT MATTERS WORK FOR YOU

✓ Sort out your needs. Write them down.

✓ Define and prioritise your objectives. Write them down.

✓ Review your aims regularly.

✓ Decide whether you want to generate income, or protect your capital, or try to do both.

✓ Be ready to change and try to keep your investments flexible.

✓ Make a list of questions about any investment. Use it as a checklist.

2 Evaluating the Risk/Reward Relationship

There is no reward without risk.

1 UNDERSTANDING THE RISKS

2 JUDGING THE RISK PROFILE

3 SPREADING THE RISK

4 BALANCING THE RISK/REWARD EQUATION

things that
really matter

When making your plans, you must decide about the degree of risk you are happy with. This does not mean that it is set in concrete. You may change your attitude at different times of your life, or depending on how much money you have to invest. Remember – review your circumstances regularly and be ready to change your plan if necessary.

To make an informed judgement about the risk attached to an investment, you need to know what to look for, and understand what your money is going into. Don't be lulled into a false sense of security by the word 'guaranteed'. Find out exactly what the guarantee is.

Remember: If you expect a return on your money, there can be no such thing as an absolute, watertight, 100 per cent risk-free investment.

IS THIS YOU?

● *I want to eliminate all element of risk – whatever the cost.* ● *I want to try to protect my capital against the effects of inflation.* ● *I would like to invest in some company shares, but I don't have enough money to risk losing it all.* ● *I have enough to invest in companies, but I don't know whether to back my judgement or play safe by investing in a unit trust.* ● *I have sufficient money to put some in slightly higher risk investments in the hope of getting a higher return.*

UNDERSTANDING THE RISKS

You must know what you are investing in if you are to understand the risk factor. Some of the most common forms of investment are:

● **Lending money**. You lend money to somebody or some organisation, and they pay you interest. You can lend to the government (a low-risk environment), or to banks, by having money on deposit, to companies, or to an individual. Loans can be secured (i.e. you have some claim on property if the borrower defaults) or unsecured.

● **Equity shares in companies**. You become a part owner of the company, and share in the risks and rewards of that company. This has a higher risk profile than loans, but the rewards are potentially greater.

● **Collective investments** (unit trusts, investment trusts or open ended investment companies). You invest in a larger fund which then invests in a much wider range of companies than you could afford to. You are reducing the risk element by spreading your investment.

- **Property**. You buy land and buildings – something very concrete. You get income from the people who rent it from you, and the property may increase in value.

Know what you are getting yourself into. If you are in any doubt – give it a miss.

 JUDGING THE RISK PROFILE

There are some obvious pointers to the risk element.

Your assessment of risk is coloured by the **quality of the information**. This depends on the trust and confidence you have in the person giving you the information. Information always comes from someone, whether it is the man in the pub, or from the pages of the *Financial Times*.

If you are at all uncertain, try to corroborate the information with someone in whom you have confidence.

You cannot have too much information.

All forms of saving and investment have something behind them. Take, for instance, a building society account. By saving in this you are putting money into a large pool which is then loaned to people buying a house. That is very simple to understand. Other forms of investment may not be quite so transparent. A name such as General Amalgamated Consolidated Portfolio PLC does not really give any clue as to what your money would be invested in. Is it a chain of seedy nightclubs? Is it an international group exploiting the resources of the third world?

A further indicator of risk is the **size of the company or fund into which you are investing**. Take the example of a unit trust.

- What is the size of the fund?

- Is it several millions?
- Or is it tens of millions?

When you know how big the fund or company is, you can make your own decisions. Investment is one area where big may be beautiful. However, smaller companies or funds can provide better performance.

Size matters.

Another factor in judging the degree of risk attached to a particular investment is **the extent of marketability**. The ultimate in marketability for company shares is the Stock Exchange. Shares in quoted companies may be sold openly to any other willing buyer. The number of transactions on the Stock Exchange runs into millions every week.

At the other end of the scale, it would not be easy to find a buyer for shares in a small family company. In general terms, shares in smaller companies are not so marketable as shares in bigger companies.

If you can't sell it, don't buy it.

Decide whether your investment is going to be **short term or long term**. This will affect the risk.

If you invest long term, you must take into account the effects of inflation. This is obviously not so important for the short term.

- If you want to put some money away for one year or less, then a deposit with a bank or building society represents a low-risk investment.

For the same length of time, investing in shares would be a high risk – you could well make a loss, especially when dealing costs are taken into account. If you invest long term, then a deposit in a bank or building society would be a high risk. It would be virtually certain that the capital invested would be worth less in, say, ten or fifteen years' time than it is now. Inflation will have eroded the purchasing power of the money.

- Investing in shares for the long term still has a risk factor, but not as great as for the short term. Historically, prices of shares have at least kept up with inflation.

Inflation affects the long-term risk.

 SPREADING THE RISK

As far as possible, **spread the risk**. If you invest all your money in one company and it goes bust, you will lose everything. If that company represents only 5 per cent of your invested money, you will not be completely wiped out.

Consider putting your money into different types of investment. Some might go in unit trusts, some in a bank or building society, some into property of some sort. Often, when one type of investment is doing badly another is doing well.

If you do not have enough money to have shares in many different companies, a collective investment of some sort makes sense.

Never put all your eggs in one basket!

 BALANCING THE RISK/REWARD EQUATION

When you have made your assessment of the risks involved, you can then apply your own judgement of how much risk to take when making your investments. If you have enough money, you may decide to put some in low-risk, some in medium-risk, and some in high-risk investments.

If you are happy to take a degree of risk, at least with some of your money, look at the best returns available within that risk band.

If you decide that your money should be in low-risk investments and savings, look very carefully at the degree of safety. If there are any 'guarantees', find out exactly what is guaranteed. Then, within these guidelines, find the best return you can get for your money.

The equation will always be – lower risk = lower rewards; higher risk = higher rewards.

MAKING WHAT MATTERS WORK FOR YOU

✓ Find out all you can about the investments you are considering.

✓ Make your judgement of the risk profile of each investment.

✓ Spread your risk as much as possible.

✓ Decide whether you want to split your money into different risk profiles. Make a decision – and go for it!

3   Tackling the Stock Market

*When you know where you are going, the Stock
Market can be like Aladdin's cave.*

5

things that
really matter

1 DEALING IN STOCKS AND SHARES

2 CHOOSING A STOCKBROKER

3 GETTING YOUR PORTFOLIO MANAGED

4 UNDERSTANDING THE INDEX AND READING THE PRICES

5 SPOTTING A GOOD THING

The stock markets of the world bring together willing
buyers and sellers to deal in all sorts of investments.
However, they hold for some people a kind of mystique that
makes them inaccessible.

The London Stock Exchange (and indeed all stock
exchanges in the world) was set up to provide a place for
people wishing to trade company shares. The growth of
limited liability companies produced a need for shareholders
to be able to buy or sell shares. Without this facility, far
fewer people would have been willing to invest in
companies.

*Once you understand what the Stock Market is all about, it can
become the backbone of your savings strategy.*

IS THIS YOU?

● A friend gave me a tip about some shares that should do well. I don't know how to go about it.
● I don't know the difference between shares, stocks, government securities, unit trusts, etc. ● I have heard that over the long term equities proved by far the best investment. How do I invest my money in them? ● I don't know if it is safe to entrust my shares to a stockbroker.

① DEALING IN STOCKS AND SHARES

- **Market makers** are dealers in stocks and shares. They only deal with stockbrokers. A broker will approach a market maker stating that he wants to deal in a quantity of a certain share. The market maker will quote a buying price and a selling price. If the broker is satisfied, he will tell the market maker whether he wants to buy or sell, and the quantity.

- **SETS** is a computerised system which at present only caters for dealing in the shares of the top 100 shares on the Stock Exchange. Through this system stockbrokers offer to buy or sell certain quantities of shares at certain prices. The computer then matches up buyers and sellers.

- **Stockbrokers** deal with members of the public. You approach the stockbroker with your request. He will tell you the price, and if you agree, he will go ahead with the transaction. He will send you a contract note showing the number of shares, the price of the deal, his commission and expenses. If you have bought, you must pay the amount due within five working days. If you have sold, the stockbroker will pay you within five working days.

When you understand how the Stock Market works, you can see where you fit in.

 CHOOSING A STOCKBROKER

It is not too difficult to find a stockbroker. They are in business, and will not turn away the right sort of client. The best introduction is through a friend or relative who can tell you how good they feel the service is. An accountant or solicitor can also probably recommend a stockbroker.

Once you have found a stockbroker stay with them unless there is a serious problem.

The stockbroker can offer one of three types of service:

- **Advisory**. The stockbroker advises you when you want to buy or sell. They may also advise at other times.

- **Execution only**. The stockbroker will only act on your instructions. They may have no opinion on your decision, or advise against it. But if you give the order to go ahead, they will carry out your request.

- **Discretionary**. The stockbroker will make any deals which they think are right for you.

Find a stockbroker – preferably by recommendation – and stick with them.

 GETTING YOUR PORTFOLIO MANAGED

A stockbroker will manage for you a **portfolio of shares** provided that it is of reasonable size. They would send you a valuation and update it, typically once or twice a year. The valuation will show a summary of your investments by sector (e.g. banking, manufacturing, insurance etc.), and analysed geographically.

The stockbroker's expertise can be extremely beneficial – and the cost to you is usually minimal.

 UNDERSTANDING THE INDEX AND READING THE PRICES
The most widely regarded indexes are those published by the *Financial Times*. Perhaps the most commonly quoted is the FTSE 100 Index – an index of the top 100 shares traded on the London Stock Exchange. The *Financial Times* also publishes the All Share Index, the Ordinary Share Index, the Non-Financials Index, the UK Government Securities Index, and the FT World Index.

These show the movement of the shares which make up that particular index. They are often shown as graphs, with the familiar troughs and peaks. They can be used as points of comparison. For example, the price movement of a share can be compared to the movement in the FTSE 100 Index. Or the index can be used to show a correlation between share prices and other indicators such as interest rates.

You cannot have too much information.

Most newspapers publish a list of prices of shares. The most complete one is in the *Financial Times*. Listings will group shares by sector, i.e. banks, chemicals, insurances, industrials, etc. A typical listing will show:

- **The price** – the middle price at the close of business on the previous day.

- **+ or –** – the movement in price from the day before.

- **High/Low** – the highest and lowest price over a period – usually the last 52 weeks.

- **Yield** – the rate of return you would get if you bought at the price quoted.

- **P/E** – the price/earnings ratio. This shows the price of the shares expressed in relation to the earnings of the company.

- **Market capitalisation** – the total number of shares in issue multiplied by the current price.

Keep regular tabs on your shares.

 SPOTTING A GOOD THING

Blue chips is the name given to top companies – broadly speaking, the ones in the FTSE 100 Index. These companies have the soundest financial base, and a strong track record. But things can go wrong, and there have been spectacular failures of blue chip companies. However, blue chips are usually the safest amongst equities.

Key indicators. When looking for a good investment, the following factors are important:

- *Market sector*. Choose which part of the economy you would like to invest in. If you feel, for instance, that leisure industries will be strong in the future, that is the sector to look in.

- *Price/Earnings ratio*. This important indicator shows how many years' profits are represented by the share price. Always compare the P/E ratio with other companies in the same sector.

- *Dividend yield*. This is the actual rate of return you will get at present dividend rates. Check that this is not out of line too much with the average for the sector.

- *Earnings growth*. This is a measure of how well the company's performance has improved over the recent past. Always look for steady growth.

- *Quality of earnings.* Past information is not as important as future earnings. The quality of earnings is the term given to market sentiment. City analysts form opinions about the company. If they have doubts, the quality of earnings is said to be low.

Keep looking for good investment opportunities. You will develop a 'nose' for these things.

MAKING WHAT MATTERS WORK FOR YOU

✓ If you are going into the Stock Market, make sure you know how it works and learn the wrinkles.

✓ Take your time in choosing a stockbroker. If you click, stay with them. Decide whether you want an advisory, execution only, or discretionary service, and always listen to your stockbroker's advice.

✓ Take an active interest in your shares. If you have a large enough sum to invest you can make the most of your stockbroker's expertise by having your portfolio managed.

✓ Keep track of the index, and review your portfolio regularly.

✓ Know what makes a good investment, and be willing to back your own judgement.

4 Choosing a Collective Investment

Collective investments are the best way to spread your risk with limited money.

3
things that
really matter

1 **UNDERSTANDING THE FORMAT**

2 **JOINING AN INVESTMENT CLUB**

3 **CHOOSING A FUND**

Investing in the Stock Market may be a good thing, but what if you do not have enough money to make a portfolio? Collective investments take relatively small amounts of money from many people and pool the money to invest in a large number of companies.

Collective investments work on the principle of reducing risk by allowing you to invest in many different companies. You may not be able to have a wide variety of shares or other investments if you have limited capital. A large number of people invest a relatively small amount into one 'pot' (the fund) and the fund is invested in a larger range of investments than each individual could do alone.

The risk is spread, and the fund managers are able to manage the fund actively, to achieve the best results.

IS THIS YOU?

- *Should I invest in stocks and shares or unit trusts?*
- *I don't know the difference between unit trusts and investment trusts. Does it really matter?* • *Is it worth investing in unit trusts as well as shares?* • *If I have enough money to invest in a good portfolio of shares, is there any point in investing in unit trusts as well?*

UNDERSTANDING THE FORMAT

There are several forms of collective investment. The most common are:

- unit trusts
- investment trusts
- OEICs

What is the difference, and does it really matter?

Unit trusts

These are funds which **accept money from investors to invest in companies**. There are over 150 authorised unit trust groups in the UK and thousands of funds to choose from.

Legally, a unit trust is governed by a trust deed. This creates a trust between the trustees (the people who are entrusted to safeguard the money) and the managers. Legally, the fund is not owned by the investors, but by the trustees for the benefit of the investors. The actual management of the investments is done by the fund managers.

When a unit trust receives new money from you, it creates new units in the fund. When you wish to cash in your investment, the unit trust pays out the money and cancels the units. This is the main difference between unit trusts and investment trusts. This feature means that it is an 'open-end fund'. The price of units in each fund is quoted daily in the financial press and in the financial pages of daily newspapers. The prices are updated daily and are arrived at by totalling the values of all the shares owned by the fund, and dividing that between the number of units in issue. This is another difference between unit trusts and investment trusts.

Investment trusts

These are limited liability companies, and are quoted on the Stock Exchange. They have a limited capital, and if you wish to buy shares in an investment trust **you have to buy the shares on the Stock Exchange**. This feature means that it is a 'closed-end fund'. It also means that a shareholder is the legal owner of a proportion of the company's assets.

The investment trust invests in other companies, in much the same way that unit trusts do. Usually, however, the investment trust does not act as an 'umbrella' with several funds. Each investment trust has its own investment strategy, and invests within its plan.

The price of the shares is determined in the same way as prices of other shares – by supply and demand. Thus, the total value can be arrived at by multiplying the price by the total number of shares in issue. This is known as the market capitalisation. By comparing this with the market value of all the shares which the company owns (its investments), you can arrive at a generally used indicator for investment trusts. It is common for the shares of an investment trust to stand at a discount to the value of the shares it holds as investments. The amount of this discount is an indicator of market sentiment towards the investment trust.

OEICs

This stands for 'Open-Ended Investment Companies'. As the name suggests, an OEIC combines the open-ended nature of unit trusts with the company legal structure of investment trusts. A particular feature of OEIC is that **there is one price for both buyers and sellers**. This contrasts to both unit trusts and investment trusts, where there is a spread between the price to a buyer and the price to a seller.

Decide what format you want to use.

 JOINING AN INVESTMENT CLUB

A more informal type of collective investment, an investment club consists of a number of people getting together (usually on a regular basis) to make their investment plans. Obviously, as the number of people involved is much smaller there is not so much money to invest, and the members are usually amateurs. However, it does give the members **a more direct say in the investment of their money**.

Because money is involved, it is necessary to have rules and a proper control system to safeguard the money and investments.

The development of the Internet has also seen the emergence of 'investment clubs' on the net. These are more informal, because the club members only exchange information and tips, rather than pooling their money.

Investment clubs can be a good way of 'having a go' and meeting other like-minded people.

 CHOOSING A FUND

You are now ready to make an investment in a collective

fund. What is available to you, and how should you decide? There are many funds available, but most fall within the following main categories:

Growth Funds aim to provide capital growth. They produce a lower income, and can be considered a slightly higher risk profile than income funds.

Income Funds are geared to produce an income which has a realistic possibility of growing each year at least to keep pace with inflation. In theory, the capital growth potential should not be so good on these funds, but historically they have shown good capital growth.

High Income Funds are geared to produce a higher than average income, but this will not have as realistic a chance of increasing each year in line with inflation as pure income funds. The additional income is generated by mixing ordinary shares with various fixed interest investments in the form of government stocks, preference shares, debentures, etc. Obviously, the opportunities for capital growth are more restricted.

Geographical Funds invest in a particular area of the globe. Typical funds might be 'Far East', 'American', 'Pacific', 'European', 'Eastern Europe', or 'Emerging Markets'. These funds should be considered higher risk, and you should approach them with only as much confidence as you have in the economies of those geographical areas.

Ethical Funds either avoid certain negative factors, or actively invest in certain positive factors. These are funds for true believers. See Chapter 9.

Split Capital Funds are funds in which the units or shares are in two classes – income or capital. One class gets all the capital growth, the other all the income.

Small Companies Funds sometimes called 'Opportunity Funds', invest in smaller companies which the managers believe have good growth opportunities. They are a higher risk investment, but carry the opportunity for high capital growth.

Tracker Funds 'track' the movement of various Stock Market indexes. They do this by investing in the same companies whose shares are included in the index concerned. These funds do not rely on active trading by the managers, since the investments are relatively stable and unchanging. Investments are only bought or sold when there is any change to the investments included on the index used. The annual management fee on these funds is therefore usually considerably lower than other types of funds and many people invest in them for this reason.

Fund of funds: these invest in other unit trusts or investment trusts. This spreads the investment risk even further, and they can be considered a lower risk investment. However, because of the wide spread of investments, the income performance is not usually spectacularly good.

Gilt and Fixed Interest Funds are invested in government securities and other fixed interest stocks. They provide a spread of risk for those who wish to obtain the best fixed interest returns available.

Corporate Bond Funds are invested in company fixed interest borrowings, such as bonds and debentures. They are most common in the Personal Equity Plan (PEP) products. They offer a high return but very limited capital growth.

Understand each type of fund fully before you invest in it.

MAKING WHAT MATTERS WORK FOR YOU

✓ If you do not have enough money for a share portfolio of your own,
  collective investments can put your money in a large number of
  different companies. They provide a good way to spread your risk, and
  get professional management of your investments.

✓ If you want to 'have a go' yourself try joining an investment club.

✓ Look carefully at the type of collective investments available and
  choose as many different types as you can.

5 Investing in Your Country

*'As safe as the Bank of England.' Investing in
your country is one of the safest ways of saving.*

3

things that
really matter

1 **KNOWING WHY TO INVEST IN GOVERNMENT
STOCKS**

2 **KNOWING HOW TO INVEST IN GOVERNMENT
STOCKS**

3 **UNDERSTANDING NATIONAL SAVINGS**

Just as companies sometimes need to borrow money, so the
government also has to borrow money. It does this by
issuing loan stocks, and through National Savings. These are
really low-risk forms of investment, and are used by many
people for just that reason. Many people with a portfolio of
other investments also include a proportion in government
stocks.

*Whatever name they bear, government stocks are all basically the
same – by investing in them, you are lending the government money.*

IS THIS YOU?

● *I would like absolute safety for my money.* ● *I want to know what rate of interest I will be receiving for the foreseeable future.* ● *I want to be able to receive interest without tax being deducted at source.*

① KNOWING WHY TO INVEST IN GOVERNMENT STOCKS

They are referred to under a series of names, including the following:

- Treasury Stock
- Exchequer Stock
- Consols (short for Consolidated Stock)
- Funding Stock
- Convertible Stock
- War Loan

Government stocks are quoted on the Stock Exchange, and for those purposes they are divided into:

- short dated (up to 5 years)
- medium dated (5 to 15 years)
- long dated (over 15 years)
- undated
- index linked

The short, medium, and long dates refer to the **redemption date**. Undated stocks have no redemption date, and in theory could go on for ever. There are only three of these stocks currently in issue.

The stocks are redeemed at par (apart from the index-linked stocks). That means the repayment of the amount loaned is made on the stated date, at the same nominal amount at which they were issued. This may not be the same as the amount you paid, since their value fluctuates on the Stock Market.

Index-linked stocks have a redemption date but are not repaid at par. The amount at which they are repaid is linked to the change in the retail prices index between the issue date and the redemption date. For example, if an index-linked stock was issued when the retail prices index stood at 100, then repaid when the index stood at 200, the amount repaid would be twice the original nominal amount of the stock.

Interest is paid twice yearly on government stocks, with income tax deducted at source. If you are not liable to tax you may apply to the Inland Revenue to have the tax refunded. Most stocks have a fixed interest rate, so when you buy you get that rate of interest until the stock matures.

Government stocks produce a fixed interest, and can be mixed with shares in a balanced portfolio.

 KNOWING HOW TO INVEST IN GOVERNMENT STOCKS

As government stocks are quoted on the Stock Exchange, you can buy them through a stockbroker in a similar way to shares.

Buying government stocks on the National Savings Register

As an alternative to the Stock Exchange, you may buy government stocks from National Savings. There is a small charge, but it is not usually as much as buying on the Stock Exchange. The other main advantage of buying them this way is that the interest is paid gross – i.e. with no income tax deducted – although it is taxable. This is often the preferred option for those who are not liable to income tax. The majority of government stocks are on the National

Savings Register and available to buy in this way.

Prices of government stocks

Government stocks are quoted on the Stock Exchange, at a figure for which you may buy or sell £100 worth of the nominal value of the stock.

Any particular stock can be priced over 100, in which case it is said to be at a premium, or under 100, which is said to be at a discount. The price is governed by the prevailing interest rates. For example, if prevailing interest rates are around 8 per cent, and the nominal interest rate is 12 per cent, the demand for that stock is likely to be high, and the price will rise above 100. In fact, unless the stock had a very short life to redemption, the price would rise to about 150, so that the yield would be roughly equivalent to the prevailing rates.

Yields

The financial press, in quoting prices for government stocks, gives yield figures. This means the actual return you will get on your money and, unless the price is 100, it will be different from the nominal interest rate of the stock. However, there are two yields quoted:

- **Interest yield** – the actual yield which you would receive on your money if you invested. This is simple to see, as in the example given above. If a stock with a nominal interest rate of 12 per cent is quoted at 150, the interest yield will be 8 per cent.

- **Redemption yield** (quoted for all but undated stocks) is an additional indicator. It can be calculated because government stocks have a fixed redemption date. It represents the 'real' yield you would get over the remaining life of the stock. In other words, it takes into account the premium or the discount in the price.

The redemption yield has been called the 'real' yield, because it is important to bear this factor in mind when comparing prices and yields. It is shown at its most extreme in very short dated stocks. For example, in July 1997, the following price appeared in the financial press: '*Exchequer 15% 1997 – price 102.5 – interest yield 14.63% – redemption yield 6.62%*'. With the price at 102.5, it might have appeared a good bargain to buy a 15 per cent stock. But the stock was dated 1997, and only had a few months to go before redemption – in fact, there was only one more half-yearly interest payment due. This meant that in a few months' time, the stock for which you had paid 102.5 would be redeemed at par – i.e. at 100.

The redemption yields of stocks with similar life spans are very similar, even though the interest yield may be quite different.

Buy stocks either through the Stock Exchange or the National Savings Register. Be aware of the redemption yield.

 UNDERSTANDING NATIONAL SAVINGS

National Savings are also a government department, and when you invest in National Savings you are again lending money to the government. National Savings have several different products:

- **National Savings Bank Ordinary Accounts** – available at post offices, paying a low rate of interest. However, the first £70 per year of interest is tax free.

- **National Savings Bank Investment Accounts** – also available at post offices, giving a slightly higher rate of interest, paid gross, but liable to tax.

- **National Savings Certificates** – certificates which mature after five years. You can buy fixed interest certificates, or index-linked certificates. These give tax-free income, but only when the certificate matures.

- **Premium Bonds** – do not give any interest, but go into a prize draw every month, for tax-free prizes, up to £1 million each month.

- **National Savings Income Bonds** – give monthly interest, paid gross, but liable to tax. Three months' notice is required to cash them in.

- **National Savings Capital Bonds** – have a life of five years. Interest is added each year to the value of the bond. You must hold them five years to get the full benefit of the interest. Interest is credited gross, but taxable.

- **National Savings Pensioners' Guaranteed Income Bonds** – available to people over 60 years of age. They pay a fixed rate of interest for five years, paid gross each month, but the interest is taxable. You can cash them in early, but with a penalty on the interest.

- **National Savings FIRST Option Bonds** – fixed rate bonds which pay interest with tax deducted at source. The interest is added to the value each year. You have the option of renewing them on each anniversary.

- **National Savings Children's Bonus Bonds** – fixed interest bonds with a five year life. At the end of the term, an extra bonus is added on. They may only be taken out by adults for the benefit of children.

National Savings give a wide range of products suitable for most circumstances. They can form part of any savings strategy.

MAKING WHAT MATTERS WORK FOR YOU

✓ You do not have to be particularly patriotic to invest in government securities.

✓ If you have enough money, government stocks can and should form part of your total portfolio.

✓ Understand the structure of the various issues of government stocks. If you are better off receiving interest gross, buy your government stocks through the National Savings register.

✓ You can use National Savings to suit various circumstances.

6 Planning for Your Retirement

You are never too young to start saving for retirement.

4

things that
really matter

1 **JOINING A SUPERANNUATION SCHEME**

2 **TAKING OUT A PERSONAL PENSION PLAN**

3 **CHOOSING A POLICY**

4 **TAKING THE BENEFITS**

The basic state pension does not given an adequate income for most people's expectations. There are tax incentives to provide for retirement – the government knows that it must encourage people to save for their retirement. Many people put off thinking about saving for their retirement, but this is the most dangerous thing you can do. If there was just one golden rule of saving for retirement, it would be this – **do it now!**

When you come to take your pension benefits, there are many options available, and this is when advice from a professional can be very useful. The options are somewhat complex, and the long-term effects can be quite considerable.

Your retirement is the longest holiday you will have. Make sure you provide adequately to enjoy it.

IS THIS YOU?

• I don't know whether to join my employer's pension scheme or take out a personal pension.
• I only have a couple of years until I retire. Is it too late to start saving for my retirement? • I have only just started work. Is it too early to save for my retirement? • I am just retiring. How should I take the benefits of my retirement plan?

① JOINING A SUPERANNUATION SCHEME

Many employers have retirement schemes of one sort or another. These schemes may be **contributory or non-contributory**. You may have to serve a period of time before you qualify to join the scheme, but persevere – it is worth it. In addition to the amounts you contribute, your employer will make a contribution. For this reason alone an employer's scheme is nearly always better than taking out a personal pension scheme. You can, however, still make additional voluntary contributions to top up your pension provision.

Always join your employer's scheme when it is offered.

② TAKING OUT A PERSONAL PENSION PLAN

If you are self-employed, or in an employment which does not have a pension scheme, you may be eligible to join a **personal pension scheme**. You must have qualifying earnings – either from self-employment, employment, or furnished holiday lettings. You get tax relief on your contributions. You may take the benefits at any time between the ages of 50 and 75, unless you are in a specialised occupation which has agreed earlier retirement ages.

You may take part of the benefits as a tax-free lump sum, but most of the fund must be taken as a pension for the rest of your life.

A personal pension plan can be the best long-term investment there is.

 ### CHOOSING A POLICY

There are many types of policy, and many salesmen trying to sell you their company's policy. Think about the following:

Basis of fund growth

The main types of policy are unit linked or with profits.

Unit linked means that your premiums buy a certain number of units in the pension fund. The value of the fund is the market value of those units at any time. The market prices can fluctuate considerably – so the timing of the retirement date could be quite critical.

With profits means that the investment profits each year are added to your pension, in the form of a 'bonus declaration'. Once added, these bonuses cannot be taken away, no matter what happens to the value of the underlying fund. The ups and downs are smoothed out, and in good years, some of the profit is kept back to even out the poor years. At the retirement date, a terminal bonus is also added. This is subject to more fluctuation than the annual bonuses, and can make up a large part of the fund at retirement.

Flexibility

Do you want to pay regular premiums, or a series of single premiums? Does your policy allow you to suspend premiums if necessary? If you are paying regular premiums, can you add single premiums later?

Charging structure

Most companies pay commission. Regular premium policies usually show a large deduction in the first couple of years of the policy to cover the commission. This is known as 'front end loading'.

Death before retirement

Always find out what would happen if you should die before taking the pension benefits. You should always look for the fund value to be paid to your estate, not just a return of premiums, even if interest is paid.

Consider all these factors carefully – if necessary, get some independent advice.

 TAKING THE BENEFITS

When you take the benefits, you have several options:

Tax free cash – always take the maximum cash benefit that you can. This lump sum can then be invested.

Open market option – all companies must give you this, which means that you can take the value of your fund, and get a pension quote from another company. Pension rates do vary, and if your fund is quite big, it is worthwhile scanning the market for the best deal.

Income drawdowns – if annuity rates are not good at the date you retire, you may defer taking the full benefits from your fund. Instead, you may 'draw down' a certain amount from the fund each year (within limits) until you take the benefits, or reach the age of 75.

Phased retirement – if you have enough in your pension fund, or you have a series of pension funds, you may be able to phase in your retirement. This means that you start to take a proportion only of the benefits, and gradually built up to the full benefits. This is useful if you want to start working less before you retire.

Pension benefits – you may get quotes for the annuity for the rest of your life on several bases. It may be a fixed amount, or an escalating amount. If escalating, it may escalate by a fixed percentage, or be linked to inflation. It may have a guarantee of being paid for a number of years, even if you die early, or it may be without guarantee. It may be for your life, or for the joint lives of you and your spouse. You can also get better rates for an 'impaired life expectancy' – i.e. if you have a life-threatening illness.

The best benefits in the long term are not always the best immediate benefits.

MAKING WHAT MATTERS WORK FOR YOU

✓ Join your employer's scheme if you can.

✓ Start saving as soon as you can – you are never too young. Make full use of any tax incentives.

✓ Look carefully at the basis of your policy. Use as many different policies as you can afford.

✓ When taking the benefits, take as much cash as possible. Get the best long-term benefits when retiring – don't just live for today.

7   Benefiting from Incentives

Never let the incentive tail wag the investment dog.

1 BENEFITING FROM TAX BREAKS

2 GETTING SHAREHOLDER CONCESSIONS

things that
really matter

Incentives exist on several types of investment, the most obvious being a tax exemption in some form or other. However, incentives should never be the sole reason for making a certain type of investment. In fact, make it a general rule that you look only at the other aspects of an investment (risk, etc.) to decide whether it is right for you.

Only after that should you look at incentives. If all other criteria are similar, then if one investment offers an incentive, it would make it more attractive than another without incentives.

Remember to evaluate the risk/reward relationship before being persuaded by an incentive.

IS THIS YOU?

● I don't really understand tax, but I have heard that there are some investments which can save me tax. ● I know a little about tax incentives, but I don't know if the risk element is greater. ● How can I find out what companies offer extra incentives on owning their shares?

BENEFITING FROM TAX BREAKS

Some types of investments and savings benefit from tax incentives. Here are some that do:

National Savings Bank Ordinary Account – the first £70 of interest each year is exempt from income tax.

National Savings Certificates – the interest and index-linking increases on National Savings Certificates are exempt from income tax and capital gains tax.

Government securities – most are exempt from capital gains tax on any profit made on selling them.

Individual Savings Accounts – a form of tax-free savings introduced in April 1999:

● You may invest up to £5,000 per year, with an extra allowance of a further £2,000 in 1999/2000, making a maximum possible £7,000 investment in 1999/2000.

● Of this, up to £1,000 (£3,000 in 1999/2000) may be in the form of cash deposits (i.e. in a bank or building society account), and up to £1,000 may be invested in life assurance.

● There is a maximum lifetime investment limit of £50,000.

● An ISA may include any combination of cash, stocks and shares, unit trusts, life assurance and National Savings.

- There will be no minimum 'lock in' period. You will be able to cash in your ISA at any time.

- There are plans to market the new ISAs through supermarket cash desks.

- You will be able to transfer existing PEPs and TESSAs into the new ISAs.

Pensions – the government encourages people to provide for their retirement by giving tax incentives to the premiums paid. At present, you get full tax relief at the top marginal rate of income tax to which you are liable. When the pension becomes payable, some of the pension fund may be commuted to a tax-free lump sum instead of being paid as a pension. The present limit for this is 25 per cent of the fund, for personal pension plans.

Capital Gains Tax Reinvestment Relief – if an asset has been sold producing a gain chargeable to Capital Gains Tax, the gain may be deferred by reinvesting the proceeds of sale (or sometimes a smaller amount) into ordinary shares in unquoted companies. A company is unquoted if it is not quoted on a recognised Stock Exchange or on the Unlisted Securities Market, although it can be quoted on the Alternative Investment Market. Some investment houses specialise in recommending those companies which qualify for the reinvestment relief.

Friendly Societies – are allowed to issue 'tax exempt life or endowment policies'. There is a limit of £25 per month (or £270 yearly) on the premiums payable. However, within this modest amount, all the gains are free of any tax.

Employee share schemes – are designed to encourage employee loyalty. The schemes reward employees when, as a result of their work, the company performs well. They allow employees to save regularly and buy shares in the company at a discounted rate. The gains on the shares are free from tax.

Tax incentives can be a useful way of adding an extra dimension to an investment.

 GETTING SHAREHOLDER CONCESSIONS

Some companies offer shareholders concessions, usually in the form of discounts on the company's products or services. Some of these require a minimum shareholding, and some offers are for limited periods.

If you use one company's services or products often, you may find the concessions useful. For example, if you travel frequently to the Continent, you may find it useful to take advantage of Eurotunnel's or P&O's discounts to shareholders on fares.

Do not let incentives override a decision taken on otherwise purely investment criteria.

MAKING WHAT MATTERS WORK FOR YOU

✓ Make sure you understand the nature of the tax incentives available but take advantage of them only when you are sure the investment decision is right for you.

✓ Similarly, shareholder concessions will only be of benefit to you if the investment is the best for you.

8 Investing in Property

Bricks and mortar are a sound part of any
overall investment strategy.

4

things that
really matter

1 **INVESTING IN COMMERCIAL AND INDUSTRIAL PROPERTY**

2 **INVESTING IN RESIDENTIAL PROPERTY**

3 **INVESTING IN HOLIDAY LETTINGS**

4 **REALISING THE VALUE IN YOUR HOME**

As with any investment, the general rule of not putting all your eggs in one basket holds good. However, to invest in more than one property requires a substantial amount of money. If you have substantial funds, say in excess of £400,000, then it is possible to put together a good portfolio of investment properties.

Property investment also needs active management. If you have the time, interest, and knowledge, you could manage the property yourself. Alternatively, you could employ an agent to look after the management. You can also realise the value locked up in your home.

Generally, property is a good long-term investment, as it usually at least keeps up with inflation over time. However, there can be spells when the value stagnates, and even falls.

IS THIS YOU?

• *The sound of 'bricks and mortar' appeals to me, but I do not have a lot of money to invest in property.* • *My daughter is going to university. I'm thinking of buying a house that she can live in for three years, then I can let it out afterwards.* • *I would like to realise some of the value in my house, but is it safe?*

① INVESTING IN COMMERCIAL AND INDUSTRIAL PROPERTY

With the right circumstances, you could get from 10 per cent to 14 per cent return on commercial and industrial property. If you **employ an agent to manage the property**, don't forget that they will take their commission from the rent. Shop premises need a prime trading position to obtain the best rent.

Get a lease drawn up by a solicitor or estate agent. Protect your interests by making it a full repairing and insuring lease. Leases usually last between 7 and 14 years and generally provide for rent reviews every 3 years.

Commercial property is subject to the normal risks associated with the economy generally. In a recession, it may be difficult to re-let an empty property, or to sell the property at a realistic price.

Commercial property needs to be managed, but can provide good returns.

② INVESTING IN RESIDENTIAL PROPERTY

The return can be lower than on commercial property – perhaps around 5 per cent. Lettings are usually carried out on **shorthold tenancies** – either 6 months or a year. When letting residential property, always get references on prospective tenants. If you are letting furnished, you must comply with the Furniture and Furnishings (Fire) (Safety) Regulations. This could prove expensive. Other laws governing these lettings, including the Landlord and Tenant Acts, and the Housing Act 1988. These Acts give a great deal of protection to the tenant. If a tenant does not pay the rent, it can be a long process to get them evicted – about 6 months. You can also expect to lose your rent for that period.

Make sure that bills for utilities, telephone etc. are in the tenant's name – you don't want to be left with demands for unpaid bills after the tenant has left.

Residential property has many safeguards attached for the tenant, but can still be a good investment. It needs active management.

 INVESTING IN HOLIDAY LETTINGS

Property to let for holidays needs to be in a holiday area. Also, keep it up to acceptable standards for holiday letting, by regular and **frequent maintenance and redecoration**. The furnishings should be of a high standard, and comply with the regulations mentioned above.

Active management is vital, particularly on changeover days. An agent may be necessary to manage these properties – especially if the property is not near you.

Expect a return of 7–8 per cent on this type of property.

Holiday lettings often need active involvement – particularly on changeover days. The property and furnishings must up to high standards.

 REALISING THE VALUE IN YOUR HOME

Your home is probably the largest single investment you will ever make in your life. But it is not just an investment like any other. It is first and foremost a place to provide a safe and comfortable environment to live in.

Whilst the value of your house may increase, it does not mean anything in real terms until you can **realise the value**. If you sold your house you would have to buy another to live in. Unless you deliberately 'trade down' to a cheaper house, you would have to pay at least as much to buy another house, and also suffer the costs of buying, selling, and removing.

There are a number of ways to provide an additional income from the value otherwise locked up in your home. The present Home Income Plan market is made up of four main types of plan:

- Shared Appreciation Mortgages
- Roll-up Loans
- Home Reversion Schemes
- Home Income Plans

Whatever type of plan you are considering, you must stop to consider various things which could become problems, such as:

- Are any valuation, survey fees etc. reimbursed by the reversion company?

- Is the scheme transferable if you move house?

- Repairs and insurance – who is responsible?

- Will it affect any Social Security benefits you receive?

- What do your family think about it?

- What would happen if you took out the scheme as a single person, then married?

- What would happen if you took out the scheme as a

married couple, and one of you died?

- What would happen if a family member or friend moved in to care for you or provide companionship?

- What is the minimum age?

- What is the maximum loan to valuation?

- What is the minimum property value?

- Is there any restriction on the type of property (e.g. house, flat, maisonette)?

Realising the value in your home can be useful in later years, but you must be confident that your security is ensured.

MAKING WHAT MATTERS WORK FOR YOU

✓ Don't invest in property alone unless you have enough money to spread your risks. Remember that commercial property particularly is subject to the same cycles as the economy generally.

✓ Be prepared to use – and pay for – the right kind of professional help. Residential tenants are protected by many safeguards and you must make sure your interests as landlord are protected, too.

✓ Holiday lettings need active management and a high standard of maintenance.

✓ You may release some of the value locked up in your house, but make sure your home is secure. If in doubt – don't.

9　Playing on the Edge

Unconventional investments are not necessarily high risk, but make sure you understand them.

4 things that really matter

1　**INVESTING ETHICALLY**

2　**COLLECTING FOR PLEASURE AND PROFIT**

3　**DEALING IN COMMODITIES**

4　**TRADING IN DERIVATIVES**

There are a number of investment opportunities which are not 'conventional'. Many people fight shy of these, simply because they are unconventional. The real problem is lack of understanding.

Some years ago, a large pension fund raised a few eyebrows because it invested in an 'old master' painting. In the event, it actually made a good profit for the pension fund. If you are thinking of being unorthodox in your investments, then

- make sure you understand the thing you are investing in, and
- evaluate the risk factor.

Just because some idea does not have the usual characteristics of an investment, does not means that it cannot be used as part of your overall plans. The key is understanding what you are dealing with.

Once you are sure of your ground, have the confidence to go ahead.

IS THIS YOU?

● I am beginning to question whether I have been too conventional, and whether that has closed the door to investment opportunities which could be rewarding. ● I have strong principles and I want to make sure my investments are ethical. ● I have an interest in antique porcelain, and wonder if I could combine my leisure activities with my financial interests. ● I have heard that there could be big profits in commodities and futures trading, but I don't really understand them. Should I 'try them out'?

INVESTING ETHICALLY

There is now a large choice of '**ethical funds**'. These offer the investor with a conscience the chance to put their money where their mouth is. There are two main types – positive and negative.

Positive investments channel money into companies that promote a certain ethical or 'green' agenda. These can include:

- energy and resource conservation
- recycling
- renewable energy
- pollution control
- free range foods
- sustainable agriculture and forestry
- minimising waste
- environmental technology
- public transport
- fair trade with third world countries

Negative investments concentrate on avoiding companies which are involved in things such as:

- tobacco
- alcohol
- arms trade
- exploitation of third world countries
- heavy pollution
- animal testing
- pornography
- environmental damage

There are now many unit trusts which allow you to choose the right type of ethical investment to suit your preferences.

If you are going to invest ethically, you need to ask yourself whether it makes sense to invest only part of your money in ethical investments. The logic of ethical investment is that all your money should be invested ethically if that is where your scruples lead you. Otherwise part of your money is going into non-ethical investments.

Saving with a bank or building society can also be done ethically. The main opportunities here are with the Co-operative Bank, the Ecology Building Society, and Triodos Bank.

- **The Co-operative Bank** has two million customers, and does not deal with repressive regimes overseas, the fur trade, tobacco producers, field sports, or animal experiments for cosmetics.

- **The Ecology Building Society** specialises in lending money for socially responsible housing projects.

- **The Triodos Bank** is a Dutch bank that has been in the UK since 1995. It invests in projects which add social or environmental value.

Always remember – ethical investments are not necessarily low risk.

COLLECTING FOR PLEASURE AND PROFIT

There are probably not many who have not at some time – usually in childhood – had a collection of something, whether stamps, football programmes, teddy bears, dolls – in fact almost anything. There are many collectors who take these things seriously as adults, but other sorts of collections are often only developed in adult life – fine wines, antiquarian books, paintings and so on.

There are many sorts of collections you could make if you have a mind to. Some which have established markets are:

- political memorabilia
- antique greetings cards
- sporting equipment and memorabilia
- oriental ceramics
- carpets and rugs
- furniture
- toys
- film posters
- garden statuary
- stuffed animals and fish

This is by no means a complete list, but it gives an idea of the range of things which could make collections, and for which a market exists.

It does not take much, apart from a serious dedication to it, to make an investment out of a collection. However, collections are usually made primarily for pleasure. The investment potential should only be secondary. There are three main things to bear in mind when considering collectibles.

Knowing your subject

Most collections come about through an interest in the items – often the interest is kindled as a child, and grows in adult life. To make a collection into a serious investment, you should know your subject well. It is no use collecting, say, fine wines if you do not know which ones will improve when they are laid down, and which ones will increase in value. But do not be put off by a mystique about any subject. **If something interests you, learn more about it**.

Keeping them safe

Collectibles have an actual physical existence. That means that they need to be kept somewhere. Some may need special storage conditions, such as a cool wine cellar. Others, such as pictures, may need to be displayed and lit to be appreciated. Some items are even of such importance that they are loaned to a local or national museum for display. Many items will be of some value, and will need **protection**. This may mean special anti-burglary precautions, and for any serious collection, your normal household insurance will probably not cover it for loss or damage. You will probably have to incur extra cost in insuring it specifically.

Realising their value

Collections suffer from one obvious disadvantage – they do not produce an income. Therefore, in order to benefit from them in a financial sense, you will have to **realise their value** in some way. This could mean having to part with something you have become attached to. Bear this in mind at the outset.

Collecting can combine pleasure with profit – but you must know your subject.

③ DEALING IN COMMODITIES

Commodities include products such as coffee, cocoa, rubber, metals of all sorts – in fact, the raw materials that are used in industrial and food production. Because many of these come from abroad, and the process time to get them to the finished products can be considerable, the businesses that buy and sell them like to hedge the prices. This had led to markets growing up in which investors and speculators can **trade in the future prices** of these commodities.

The dealings take place in highly regulated environments. Outside investors can only deal through brokers, and are essentially taking a gamble on the future prices of the commodities traded in. The amounts needed to trade in these futures are not inconsiderable, and it is a high-risk area.

Commodities can produce high profits, but they can equally produce high losses. Do not dabble unless you can afford to lose the money.

④ TRADING IN DERIVATIVES

These are also known as 'options', but the term 'derivatives' can also embrace other things such as futures, contracts for differences, swaps, etc. They can appear complicated, and normally only the more sophisticated investors deal in these. Remember – do not invest in anything unless you understand it. The essence of derivatives is that **you have the opportunity to benefit (or lose) from an underlying 'position'** (such as the movement in the price of a share) without complete 'exposure' to that position. In plain language, you can benefit from an increase in a share price without actually owning the shares.

The simplest form of derivative is the option. These are agreements by which you pay a price (known as the option premium) for the right to buy or sell shares at a fixed price within a certain timescale. These agreements also limit the number of shares to be traded under the agreement.

If you do not exercise your option within the timescale, you have lost the right under that agreement. The person to whom you paid the premium keeps the money. However, if you do exercise your right, the person to whom you paid the premium must fulfil their side of the bargain.

The types of options are:

- **calls** – this gives the right to buy the shares
- **puts** – this gives the right to sell the shares
- **doubles** – this gives the right either to buy or to sell, but not both.

This form of trading is recognised on the London Stock Exchange and is called 'London's Traditional Options Market'. Shares in any company quoted on the London Stock Exchange may be the subject of a traditional options contract.

There is another market dealing in 'Traded Options'. This is a separate market in which the options are for fixed numbers of shares, with fixed expiry patterns, and a fixed scale of exercise prices. On the Traded Options market, the options themselves can be traded, rather than the underlying shares, and the range of shares on which options are traded is rather more limited than on the London Stock Exchange.

Options could be considered low to medium risk in the sense that the only money at risk is the money you have paid for the option premium. This is only a fraction of the cost of holding the actual shares. However, the option premium itself is a high-risk item, since the loss could be 100 per cent.

Only consider derivatives if you have money left over after making your 'core' investments.

MAKING WHAT MATTERS WORK FOR YOU

✓ If you are going to be unconventional, make sure you thoroughly understand the subject, especially if you are building a collection.

✓ Be willing to consider any possibility – even if it contradicts your preconceived ideas of investments.

✓ Make your 'core' investments first, then think about alternative investments. And make sure you appreciate the risk factor.

✓ If you feel strongly enough about ethical investments, be prepared to apply the same rigorous principles to *all* your investments.

10 Taking Advice

Never let yourself by rushed or pressured into an investment.

1 KNOWING WHEN TO USE AN ADVISER

2 KNOWING WHAT TO ASK

3 KNOWING WHO TO CHOOSE

things that
really matter

There are many 'financial advisers' around. Should you seek professional advice? Do they have any insights or inside information? There are independent advisers and tied agents.

Independent advisers can advise on any company's products. Since the Financial Services Act 1986, it is an offence to give investment advice without the proper authorisation. Most independent advisers are registered with the PIA (the Personal Investment Authority). This is one of several regulatory bodies under the overall umbrella of the Financial Services Authority which provides public protection.

Tied agents are representatives of one company. They can only advise on the products of that company. This does not necessarily mean that they offer worse advice than an independent adviser, but their scope is limited.

Remember that the adviser's commission will come out of your invested sum, whereas a fee can be paid separately, leaving your investment intact.

IS THIS YOU?

● I'm not sure if I need professional advice. ● I think I can back my own judgement, but I'm not sure how to go about investing. ● I think an adviser can help me, but I'm afraid they will pressure me into an investment that gives them the best commission. ● I can see why using an adviser would be a good thing, but they might charge too much.

① KNOWING WHEN TO USE AN ADVISER

Advisers can help you to **choose the right product for your circumstances**. The result of taking their advice, even taking into account the cost of their commission, can be considerably better than going it alone.

If you have a financial decision involving a significant amount, or if you are uncertain about what to do, this could be the time to use an adviser. If you find a good one you can trust, keep the contact.

An adviser can be worth their weight in gold – in the right circumstances.

② KNOWING WHAT TO ASK

The National Consumer's Council recommends that you ask the following questions of an adviser before signing up for any investment:

- Are you able to give advice on a range of companies, or are you tied to one company?

- What happens if I have to drop out early? What are the penalties?

- Can I vary my payments on a regular investment if I have to?

- If there are several alternatives which suit my needs, what is the commission you would get from each one?

- What proportion of my investment goes on charges? How does this compare with other products?

- What is the 'worst case scenario' that could happen to this product?

- What happens if the product fails or the company goes bust?

- Do you know of any other products on the market that are as good as or better than the one you are recommending?

- Can you show me any independent information on how this product compares with others on the market?

Approach the relationship with an adviser in a professional manner.

 KNOWING WHO TO CHOOSE

If you feel that you need advice, who do you turn to? The best way is to get a **personal recommendation**. Ask your friends or relatives if they have someone they can trust. If you cannot find one that way, look around locally, or through your *Yellow Pages*. Make an appointment, and explain your situation. A reputable adviser will:

- have to comply with strict regulatory requirements

- look at the whole of your circumstances, not just the immediate topic

- not try to pressure you into a quick decision.

If you feel you can trust the person, and have confidence in them, then follow their recommendations.

Don't be pressured into anything, but once you have an adviser you can trust, stay with them.

MAKING WHAT MATTERS WORK FOR YOU

✓ Decide whether you have enough knowledge or time to undertake the research yourself. If not, decide whether the investment warrants using an adviser.

✓ Work out in advance the right questions to ask so that you will have all the information you need for your decision.

✓ Meet the adviser and agree their method of remuneration. Then, when you feel confident, go ahead with their advice.